JUST ANOTHER MARTIAN CAT LIVING IN BASILDON

A POEM COLLECTION ON EXPLORING CREATIVITY AND THE WORLD

By Chris Statham

Also By

THE UGLY GLORY SERIES

THE MAN IN THE MIRROR - A collection on male mental health
FRIDAY NIGHT FEVER – A collection on booze, nightlife & the battle with sobriety
JELLIED EELS & MULTI-CULTURALISM – A collection on modern life in the UK
THIS IS WHY WE MET - A collection on dating, friends with benefits & sex workers
MY NORTH STAR - A collection on love, divorce & finding a way forward
JUST ANOTHER MARTIAN CAT LIVING IN BASILDON - A collection on exploring creativity & the world
LIFE PIRATE – A collection on life, death & all that jazz

AFRONIA SERIES

Crying for Afronia (Volume 1)
Escape from Afronia (Volume 2)
Dying for Afronia (Volume 3)
Afronia Rising (Volume 4)
Developing Afronia (Volume 5)

PROSE, POEM AND PICTURES SERIES

7 Days in 1 Week (Volume 1)
12 Months in a Year (Volume 2)
10 Years in a Decade (Volume 3)

OTHER FICTION NOVELS

18 Reflections and 3 Statements of Relief
Paperback Writer

DEDICATION

To the poets, artists, musicians and other storytellers of the world

Copyright and Disclaimer

Author – Chris Statham
Sketches by Hezdean Chinthengah
Published by **www.creativityxroads.com**
JUST ANOTHER MARTIAN CAT LIVING IN BASILDON, 978-1-7385368-2-5

CONTENTS

Contents

FORWARD

During a conversation with an unconventional Icelander, I totally reassessed how I perceived the world; I underwent a complete transformation. If you asked 99% of the globe's population, they would think he is a complete nutter, eccentric at best, but I consider him an unconventional genius for trying to push the boundaries of creativity and conventional acceptability. His screwball, revolutionary or virtuoso idea- depending on which side of the creative spectrum you come from – revolves around him burning books that he publishes if they remain unsold within 24 hours of printing. His theory of change, being, that while most books can survive hundreds of years, why not condense that into a few highly charged hours. Similar to performance art, his books come alive for a beautiful brief moment on the time-space continuum and then are no more than a fleeting thought in the entirety of time. It is the antithesis of traditional publishing. I expect the Icelander is an antichrist to novelists who decree their books to be exclusive objects of art rather than thought farts. The moral of the story, the more people you encounter the more you realise how diverse and interesting life can be.

I see this concept as a stroke of genius that bites into the very element of what makes us human. While I admit it's a screwed-up business model, but its brilliance is that it makes tangible the ying and yang, capturing the essence of permanence and impermanence. It reaches into the core of who we as humans are, that is to say, so many cling onto the religious concept of the hereafter when in reality, as far as I'm concerned, we are fragile and no more than one missed heartbeat from not being. Book burning can also be an analogy for life, though not thinking of one of the Nazi's first acts to burn Jewish books, nor Heinrich Heine's quote, "Where they have burned books, they will end in burning human beings".

A different, but very well-known business model, is the travel industry. I've been lucky enough, at time of writing, to have visited 56 countries, 15 of which have been in Africa, my home for the last 16 years. I realise how a passport and credit cards, luxuries afforded to some, can lead to a world of new experiences. Travelling encompasses a mixed bag of emotions, thoughts, hopes, dreads, dreams and nightmares, butterflies roaming innards as you board plane, train or automobile.

With that as a preamble, this poem collection delves into the art of creativity, the natural world and the transformative power of travel. The common themes are what makes us humans and, the ever-evolving relationship we have with the world, whether this is through books, plays, music and sport. Understanding the natural world and how travelling can increase one's knowledge of others as much as yourself is illuminating.

CREATIVITY

Writing takes me into a secret world where I'm god and establish rules, hold power and decide fates. This alternate reality is preferable to my everyday reality of being blown-up during an ugly divorce and a diminishing number of work-related contracts; it's very therapeutic. I love that whatever flows through my noggin during the creative process goes via the keyboard and materialises on screen and gives existence to my thoughts. For example, a Martian or a cat, perhaps a Martian feline living in Basildon could become a king for a millisecond before being crushed under a fire truck that's come to its rescue from inside a drain. The cat's skeleton is so thoroughly crushed, obliterated, that it's squeezed through the earth's crust and comes up in Fiji where it's bamboozled by the giant stone heads which creakily bend in worship to the tabby. That kind of creative writing- if a little less of an acid trip- encapsulates the freedom of expression and creativity that I truly cherish. I relish the unrestricted boundaries in this secret world of writing and which allows me to explore the depths of my imagination and embark on whimsical adventures. A realm where the ordinary becomes extraordinary, absurdity and fantasy intertwine, and where I can let my thoughts roam freely. While I'm no actor or musician I expect this creative freedom is what nurtures the spirit and provides a sense of liberation for other creatives to express themselves through their chosen medium.

Meraki

I write because I can,
poem because I want,
create because I have meraki,
love, passion and a lot of soul.

I live life,
love life,
allay mistakes and success these done equally
with absolute devotion,
undivided attention.

I get an idea,
an inspiration,
a something I saw and want to reproduce.

I want to capture the now,
the has been,
and the future in a kaleidoscope or monochrome
reality.

I draw my line in the moon,
my take on originality,
of interpretation of the real or abstract,
my muse, skill, innovation and meraki deciding
the outcome
I, a plaything to her creativity,
no rules other than those I choose to follow or
ignore,
the world,
my pallet,
sketchpad and keyboard,

I, deciphering my experiences into what others
can comprehend.

I put heart and soul into my words,
no matter how difficult a task,
the mental acrobatics I need to perform,
the discipline to scribe,
to crate fantastical worlds where I am God.

I do it with all my effort,
enthusiasm and eagerness,
with love in the labour,
for this is living meraki.

It's a pleasure,
an honour to put my thoughts into words,
to let people into my mind,
putting myself wholeheartedly into what I write.

Whatever you do in life,
whether singing or painting,
cooking or coffee-making,
tangoing,
put your soul into it,
every fibre of your body,
give it your all,
do it with devotion,
zeal,
meraki;
anything is possible,
this my creativity.

meraki (μεράκι)

(n.) the soul, creativity, or love put into
something; the essence of yourself that is
put into your work

The Storyteller

The author,
journalist,
musician,
actor,
photographer,
painter,
cake-baker or poet,
the friend who tells stories around the camp fire;
we each have our medium of choice,
all are storytellers.

Putting pen to paper,
tapping on the keyboard,
sketching an idea in our minds eye as we think of
a specific incident,
a thought,
a person,
a state of mind;
this,
the genesis of our storytelling.

We pull from experience and play with the what
has been,
what is and what might be.

We hope our listeners,
readers and watchers have their senses awoken,
that they gain a new perspective and empathize
with our characters,
with us, the storyteller.

The words are not always the story of our life-
we use artistic freedom to be the storyteller…

but the reader can still understand us,
know what we think,
what our beliefs are and how we live.

As storytellers,
we enjoy the challenge of finding an engaging
beginning,
introducing characters and their interwoven lives
before final crescendo and memorable end,
this, the challenge of being a storyteller.

In days gone by,
writing copy by hand in the glow of a candle,
a life's work was forever at the risk of wind, water and fire;
words, thoughts and theories at the capriciousness of carelessness and fate.

Now, we have all the tools of our trade:
spellcheck,
cutting and pasting.
saving drafts on external hard drives,
emailing oneself ideas before they are forgotten,
selling our finished work at the click of the shopping cart;
bringing words to life has never been easier,
but we must still find discipline and the muse.

Storytellers of yesteryear,
whether of plays, music, poems or stories,
we must respect those gone before,
for challenges faced,
creative trails blazed.

4 Types of Storytelling

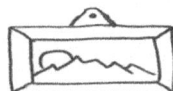

Oral   Visual   Written   Digital

The Paperback Writer

When I put pen to paper,
tap on my keyboard or sketch an idea in my
mind's eye,
I think of a specific incident,
a thought,
a person,
a state of mind.

I pull a story from my past and play with the:
what has been,
what is and what might be.

I have artistic freedom…
as a paperback writer.

A killer first sentence,
an engaging beginning,
building a plot towards a final crescendo
and memorable end.

That is the task…
of being a paperback writer.

Will you read my book of five-hundred pages,
fifteen drafts that took ten years to write,
with sleepless nights and endless proofing?

These are the physical and mental challenges
required of all paperback writers.

I'll soon be composing again.
Inscribe as I wish,
pen as I dare.
once more,
God creating worlds,
introducing characters
and interweaving lives.

I call myself,
a paperback writer.

Why do I Write?

Is it ego?
Do I think I have a new,
a unique perspective on life?

Is it the mental acrobatics of every word,
or finding meaning,
putting a thought into context that I write?

Is it developing a structure and creating a plot
with start,
middle and ending that I enjoy?

Is it the sense of achievement when writing a perfect
sentence, paragraph or chapter that flicks my switch?

Is it a way to relax,
to go into another world,
empathising with my characters for a fleeting
moment in a world of my creation,
limited only by my imagination;
is this why I create,
think and articulate?

Is it turning a concept,
a passing thought into eighty thousand words?

Is it sharing my aspirations,
frustrations,
loves,
challenges,
hopes and desires as I spill my guts on every page,
in every sentence that I crave?

Am I the protagonist in every word I write?
The female soldier?
The philanderer?
Genius?
Gangster?
Family man?
Single and free?
Child?
God?
All the above?

Are my words,
me in black and white,
my life on steroids,
a cartoon personified in every character?

But why is never one single character,
me?
Would that be too real?

Am I afraid to bare my soul,
unhide my secrets,
share my every desire,
fear,
perversion and phobia in the real world…
so hide them in my words,
my worlds?

Is writing my coward's way out,
others,
left to read between the literal and figurative lines
of my mind?

Why do I pen when writing a story is like a newly
opened jigsaw puzzle,
a picture not yet revealed?

It excites my creative spirit,
helps in my search for meraki and to understand
who I am,
this is why I write.

The Poet

I'm the addict

I drink like a fish,
fuck like a rabbit,
smoke like a chimney,
gamble as if I can afford to lose,
get high as a kite and eat like I'm starving…
but tonight my words sing to the audience;
I'm God in the worlds I create,
poetry giving me back control.

I'm the outlier

Into my fifth decade,
a business owner,
twice divorced and three estranged kids.
while I see youth and hope all around,
debts burn a hole in my pocket.
I have forgotten passions and despair crushes my
soul…
but tonight my words sing to the audience;
I'm God in the worlds I create,
poetry giving me back control.

I'm the teenager

I'm a virgin who writes about love,
who mystifies war though I've never held a gun.
A wannabe musician who silences his riffs.
In a world of uncertainty,
I write about hope when all I feel is angst…
but tonight my words sing to the audience;
I'm God in the worlds I create,
poetry giving me back control.

I'm the mother

I'm a wife to an unfaithful husband,
sister who sleeps with my sibling's boyfriend.
I hate myself,
my life,
but must keep strong for my children.
I'm the proverbial joker whose tears are those of
a clown…
but tonight my words sing to the audience;
I'm God in the worlds I create,
poetry giving me back control.

Writing Poetry

Part 1 – Writing Poetry

I like writing poems on a smartphone-
It's easy to edit and save thoughts and concepts,
stories in the minimum number of characters,
rhyming,
but not always rhythmically.

Into my poetry file I put inspiration from news
stories,
talking to friends on WhatsApp,
random word challenges;
these unavailable with pen and paper and where I
have to delve deeper into the mind for ideas and
words,
the creativity harder but reward greater as I
search for what makes sense to me as much as
my readers,
listeners.

Will they get it?
Get me?
Do I make sense?
Am I coherent in my verbiage?

Whether pen or pixel I need to be heard,
revel raw emotion,
concentration,
fixation,
sometimes abbreviation and alliteration,
always mental salvation,
I, expressing my soul,
mental levitation.

Part 2 – God, you Bastard

God,
you bastard.
Why, when I have everything,
I still want more?

God,
you bastard.
When I find happiness,
why then hit me with despair?

God,
you bastard.
Kids with cancer?
Hunger and wretchedness?

God,
you bastard.
Big fuck-off dinosaurs?
How do you explain that one?

God,
you bastard.
When I'm lucky enough to find love and friend-
ship with more than one person,
why do your Satans tell me this is impossible...
according to you?

God,
you bastard.
The holy trinity,
what's that all about?

God,
you bastard.
People kill but few find true love in your name!

God,
you bastard.
You promise everlasting harmony,
this in a worldly context of disunity.

God,
you bastard.
Water into wine,
I like your style...
so why puritanical rather than Bacchus on other
things?

God,
you bastard.
Your commandments are more about shall nots
than shalls,
of forgoing rather than enjoying;
why deny the human spirit not rejoice in it?

God,
you bastard.
Why are their many versions of you,
many gods?
Don't you know this fucks with immortals' minds?
Do you even care?

God,
you bastard.
The old testament…
were you revelling in being a bastard?

God,
you bastard.
Can you explain,
nay, justify original sin...
and not sound like a bastard?

God,
you bastard.
Are you a figment of imagination,
a psychological,
political crowd-controller?
A being we can never comprehend…
Or the very essence of what and who we are?
God,
this is your greatest trick of bastardness!

Part 3- Am I Going to Hell?

Hell,
a fiery inferno for adulterers,
killers,
all round no-gooders
blasphemers!

Will I meet those who enjoy vices that you decry,
prohibit
cause moral outrage...
or are my addictions
perversions and predilections,
peccadillos,
weaknesses...
not already a living hell?

Will you deny me the keys to the gates of heaven
for being me,
good and bad,
sometimes ugly and sad;
this what makes me human…
something You can never comprehend!

God,
with my poems,
my thoughts in words,
am I going to hell or will I become worm food,
return to the earth,
the circle and cycle of life,
my body,
nutrients for others to feast on;
my soul living on in plant and animal…
in my poems?

Inspiration

Something grabs my attention,
a thought goes through my mind,
sometimes serious,
more often flippant.

I capture those seconds,
ideas flowing from brain to pen without analysis,
the idea,
the thought,
raw,
spontaneous,
a view into my world,
a point on my time space continuum,
a mirror into my soul,
this, the start of my quest for writing poetry with
meraki.

Hemmingway

It's been a while,
poems not a lot
novel concepts many,
productive finalisation, none.

Writing in its many forms,
the spoken word or print,
ideas in black and white,
life in Technicolor glory;
thoughts readable,
this irony for all to see.

Writing,
the alphabet,
language,
not an invention or innovation,
but essential to who we are,
How we express;
wow!

A thousand words to paint one picture,
a phrase to describe a sense,
an emotion,
exhilaration,
life contemplation
fantasies and realities,
the world to consume.

I write with booze,
drink,
grog.
It opens my mind...
I don't worry about the edit but follow Heming-
way's advice.

I won't lie about my process,
my experiences good or bad as I scribe authentic.
I don't believe in right or wrong,
but that life is both full of ugly and glory.

We,
all of us,
make fuck ups and enjoy success,

we are human,
do silly shit,
that's who I am,
not fake,
won't write a sanitised version of the world,
of me.

I will keep spewing my thoughts,
life experiences,
mistakes and achievements to give others courage
to live free.

With a drink,
no hesitation to explain the what ifs and wherefores,
I mind free,
lay my life out through fiction,
poetry and pictures;
there's no place,
recess for my soul to hide.

I hope readers will examine my mind,
that they too will share their hopes and fears publicly,
with one other.

Whether through creative medium or chat,
don't live a lie,
be honest no matter how much the truth hurts.
Reveal your weaknesses,
try to find solutions,
don't be afraid,
don't live in the shadows,
you are born beautiful,
don't be too proud or ashamed of how you live,
but live free,
live your true self,
live temet nosce.

"Write drunk edit
sober"

-Ernest Hemingway

The Creative Journey

First strategy –
finish editing,
send to a publisher or agent…
and cross fingers.

Strategy number two –
self-publish,
market as best I can…
and cross fingers.

Strategy three –
try and get a Facebook following…
but how?
Cross fingers?

Let's assume I'm the most popular FB person in
the world,
ever,
1 billion followers!
How can I use this as a negotiation strategy with
agents and publishers?
How do I convince them what I bring is more
than they can offer?

Back to the how,
the toughie!
Post articles,
that might work?

Will social media readers be my target audience?
Will followers review my novels?

Should I compose poems,
little stories about me,
a view into my soul,
clues as to the type of novel I'm writing?

I could post in poetry groups,
try to reach a critical mass of followers…
however many that might be.
But is chasing a Facebook following,
me?
Am I a social-media hypocrite,
I,
normally so full of scorn for the medium?
Am I a traitor to my goal of being a paperback
writer
if I quest likes and comments?

And then I realize…
I like poetry!
To let ideas flow,
thoughts tumbling out of my head onto the page,
poem writing no longer a means but an end in
itself!

I'll soon be composing again.
Inscribe as I wish,
pen as I dare,
once more God creating worlds,
introducing characters,
interweaving lives.

I call myself a paperback writer.
a poet;
I concede defeat to the social media Chimera.

Outdoor Art

I'm in a beer garden,
many a tree,
mentally free.

The music bumping
I'm not yet jumping,
just contemplating this place of creativity,
land of opportunity,
brains not bound by structure,
politics or economy.

An idea,
inspiration,
a something I heard,
thought,
tasted,
felt,
smelt,
saw and want to reproduce.

My reason for being is to capture the now,
the has been and future.,
A kaleidoscope or monochrome reality,
as I draw a line to the moon.
My take on originality,
interpretation of the real or abstract,
my muse deciding the outcome,
I,
a plaything to her creativity where there are no rules
others than those I choose,
decide to follow or ignore,
the world my pallet,
sketchpad and keyboard,
I,
deciphering my experience into what others can
comprehend as I aim to change the politics.

Tonight, I will go with the flow,
the river of life that brought me here,
from here I will go there,
into the night unknown,
trusting my meraki to find the children of the night,
in each other delight as we go forth,
free in the mind,
to live as we dare,
to change the reality and expound a bohemian ideal.

THE Creative Anti Capitalist

Emoji Story

👩‍👩‍👧 🚫 🏩

👰🧑‍🦱⚡👨‍🦳🤔
😍⚡👨‍👧‍👦🧍
👩‍🦰🐸🍃👑
👰🔬🧍👍

🚫

🙈🧍🍃🐷
🐄🌍❤️🐚
🐄🐑🐄🐖

🚫

🍔

Let's Get Ready to Rumble

Entering the arena,
Greg,
tall, green and scaly,
his partner,
Jim,
brown, squat and hairy.

Monkey and dinosaur,
the reigning scientific champions face their theological opponents,
Adam and Eve-
created on the sixth day…
an apple their kryptonite.

What a match up, the winner,
ruler of man's mind,
for the very soul of humans,
this a conversation for the ages:
fossils or hope?
Salvation or eternal damnation?
You,
living beings,
the ultimate judge in this head-to-head

Greg,
70 million years old,
body slams Adam,
a mere 6,000;
the mortal taps out.

Monkey,
looking on,
death stares Eve,
she, secret weapon swinging,
chokes Titanosaur Argentinosaurus Huinculensis
with her snake.

Will either take a backwards step in the battle for souls?

Horse

Am I horse or stallion?
Does it matter what human shit-heads label us?
as we are equine royalty,
not donkey or ass,
but thoroughbreds who move with perfection,
power and grace.

People need us more than we them.
We gave advantage to Julius and Egyptians...
why did you turn us into Crimean cannon fod-
der?

Riding up the valley,
we were sacrificed for avarice,
slaughtered at the Somme and stuck in Passchen-
daele;
you bastards!

You bet on our finest,
make money from our sweat as our mane flows,
nostrils flare and hide perspire.

No matter how much you need us,
whether silk or tin on your head,
train and whip
you abuse us!

Our relationship must be one of partnership,
not master and commanded;
we are not lap dogs,
servile canines;
show due respect.

Acting

I feel so alive,
excited standing in front of hundreds baring my soul
as I pretend to be another.

I live a lie for two hours,
but, the reality…
I'm living my honesty.

I act my part,
this no less a fib than my daily life;
It's all a play.

My show of affection,
love for others is but a one-man show for family and friends;
I pretend happiness when all I feel is loneliness.

I was drawn to the stage as I get to be someone else,
my alter ego,
a different,
better reality to that which I'm shackled,

the limelight allowing me to be anything, everything:
a murderer, adulterer, rapist, lover…
something my life of boredom and frustration isn't!

My life on stage is more real than my reality;
is this what being an actor means?
Am I a moth drawn to flame,
the theatre,
an acceptance of my insecurity,
thespians my enablers?

Acting,
the embodiment of not being who I am but who I want to be.
Living a temporary life,
a reflection of my desires,
an embodiment of my alter-ego,
where I can be demon and angel…
just like my reality.

The Beat

A new night spot,
a live music bar no less.

It has a long and proud history;
last six-months refurbishment,
tonight, reopening;
I need to investigate.

Mellow sounds as I enter hallowed turf.
a two-tiered amphitheatre befitting the location.
Candles, ambience and dark corners,
this legendary venue's reputation well-earned.

The vocalist singing,
the drummer drumming,
guitarists strumming,
all in unity,
together,
the rise and fall of the whole greater than the
sum of its parts.

The band are family,
musical brothers and sisters,
needing each other to raise,
rise.
joint influences one goal,
one sound,
mesmeric.

The band playing,
time for floor dancing,
hips swaying,
bodies sweating and hearts racing.

I'm feeling the heat,
beat,
Reggae vibes playing,
the sound of jamming.

I'm aroused at being so alive,
living in the moment,
forgetting my past.
not thinking of tomorrow,
living in the now;
Rastafari!

Football Gods

I'm in a park,
why,
who knows;
maybe God?

Does such a beardy fella exist?
Why do I resist,
not follow convention,
always reinvention,
perhaps reincarnation as panda or brown bear,
ant or carrot,
nothing,
eaten by worms,
back to dust;
gut feeling…
that better than rust.

My mind is creating,
not disintegrating,

flaking,
slowly evaporating into the ether,
the no more tomorrow,
yesterday but a figment of imagination,
a once what had been,
a no more,
or ten perhaps more,
celebration and commiseration.

I,
my sub-conscious,
my dream leaving me high and dry trying to work
it out as the sun rises then sets,
this continuity on my time space reality,
it's never banality,
generality,
but exceptionality,
poemability,
my life but a football to the gods.

The Day Dreamer

Dreaming,
but during the day…
or is that wishing,
loving,
hoping,
wanting,
praying,
thinking and lusting,
fantasizing?

Dreaming for the girl, the boy,
the man, the woman,
ice creams, guitars, beaches,
money, wealth, fame,
toasted cheese and chutney sandwiches;
no one except the day dreamer knows.

Walking through the forest,
flying through the air,
swimming in the sea,
climbing up the mountain;
everything,
anything is possible;
no one except the day dreamer knows.

Looking at the sunset,
tasting in the kitchen,
smelling the flowers,
hearing laughter,
feeling the warmth of a body,
sensing love or hate;
no one but the day dreamer knows.

Looking on at a smile,
a frown,
a distant look the only giveaway;
the day dreamer jumping into imagination,
lost in a world of their own.

THE NATUAL WORLD & EXERCISE

What is life? What is the god damn meaning of life? The quest to this understanding has long intrigued humanity and often leaves us pondering. I have no idea of the answer so will break the question down into some fundamental aspects. What makes life apart from the literal shag in the sack? I say, it encompasses a complex interplay of elements and experiences.

There are 4 elements that define life and death, that are elemental to living, earth, air, fire and water. They ground us in the physical world and connect us to the natural rhythms of the universe. They symbolize our connection to the earth, the air we breathe, the transformative power of fire and fluidity of water. Our senses, in turn, serve as conduits through which we interact with these elements. No matter how pickled my liver is, I can still hear, smell, touch, taste and see: love is our sixth sense.

On a related matter, you've probably heard of the runner's high, the feeling of euphoria long distance runners get; what's that all about? Blood endorphin levels rise in response to exercise and endorphins are linked to positive emotions. More specifically, as blood is pumped round our grey matter, there are changes on opioid receptor activity in the pre-frontal and anterior cingulate cortex. Trust me, I needed the internet to find this information. Anyway, it's these areas of the brain which are responsible for mood regulation; with an increase in endorphins there's a corresponding increase in euphoria.

But why are we designed this way? The answer, evolution. In the early days of man moving from living in trees to roaming the savannah, we were easy prey for carnivores on the one hand and had to develop effective hunting strategies on the other. Being a biped that can sweat allowed us to go on long hunts where we could quite literally exhaust the pants of a fine looking four-legged piece of steak. Not only would our bellies be full but also feel great from our runners high, a natural painkiller to exhaustive exercise. Humans are born to run! We are designed for endurance activities and experience physiological rewards for doing so.

Combining the notions of elemental forces, our senses, and the natural highs we can experience, it becomes clear that they form the building blocks of our human existence. As such, this should be explored in poetic form to capture the very essence of what it means to be human, and invite contemplation of the grand mysteries that lie at the core of our existence.

Sixth Sense

I have all my faculties:
eyes like an eagle,
hearing like a bat,
smelling like a Labrador,
sensitive to every touch and tasting every spice.

I can't imagine life without all my senses.
What is it to be blind,
to feel you way through the world?
What is it to not know your own voice?
To not know the touch of your lover,
nor able to smell danger or experiences the tastes
of life?

Whatever befalls me,
whatever ups and downs I go through,
I give thanks for my senses.

Taken for granted
until deprived of one...
and then the body compensates!
How amazing is that?
Lose one sense...
all others get stronger.

I thank my lucky stars for my senses.
The candy stars on cakes I can see,
pick up and taste.
The fireworks that are the stars I can hear
and gunpowder smell.
The stars that are my friends and family,
who I can use all my senses to love,
this our sixth sense.

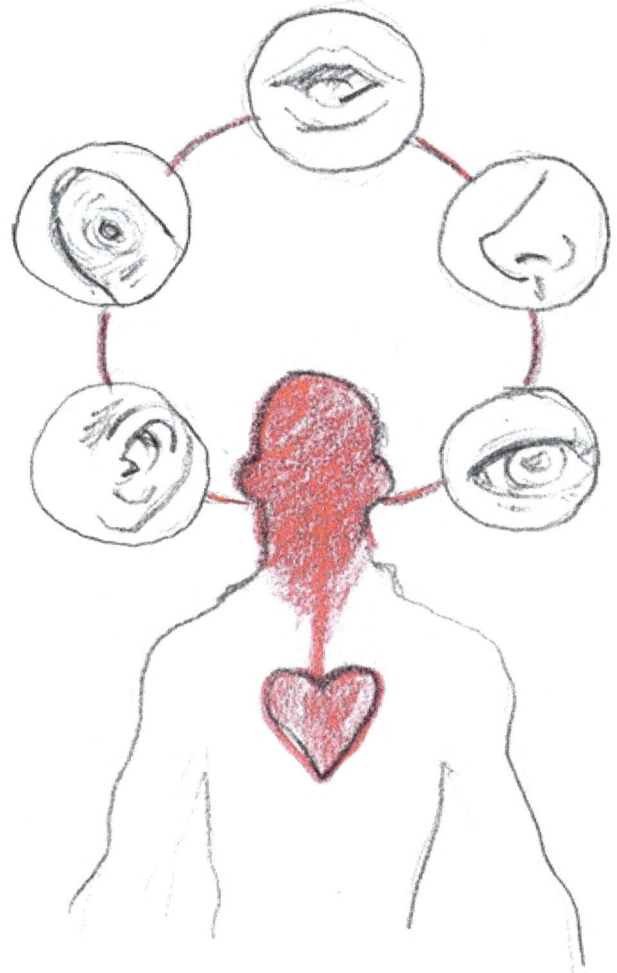

The 4 Elements

Warmth, comfort, food…
or danger, burning and destruction?

Is there fire in your heart or hearth?
Do you have a burning for love,
or will your flesh sizzle at the stake?

When on fire,
is it your skin with anticipation,
your loins burning with desire,
passion and lust or,
being burnt,
flames licking you?

Fire,
the giver and taker,
death and rebirth;
the creator of ashes from which the phoenix
rises.

Earth, air, fire and water,
the essentials to live,
the building blocks of life,
the harbingers of death.

Our eternal quest to conquer mother nature,
trying to tame the uncontrollable:
hurricane, tornado, forest fire,
earthquake, volcano or tsunami –
Gaia able to finish us on a whim.

We have hubris in unwinnable battles,
though, however big the task,
we don't shirk the challenge,
but rather try,
fail and try again!

This is what makes us human –
the drive to prevail against all odds.
thrive in spite of disasters,
be comfortable in mind, body and soul.

Fire
What do you think,
when you think of fire?

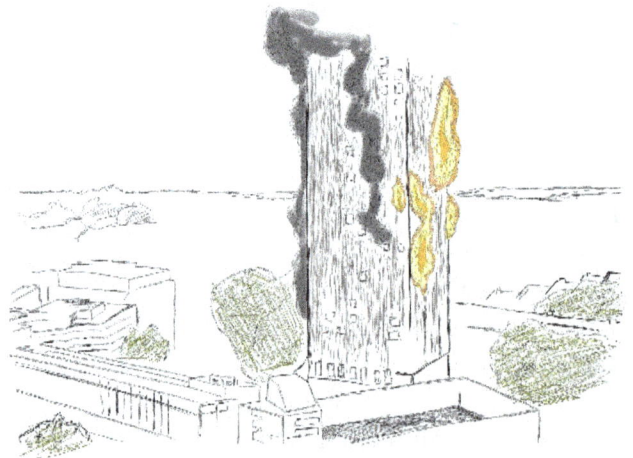

Water

Ice,
steam,
flowing water;
an amazing trinity.

From the smallest ripple in a pond,
or drip from a tap,
to the largest stream, river, lake, sea, ocean or

tsunami,
water is the giver and taker of life.

Nothing better on a summer's day,
nothing worse on a winter's night.
We can't live without water so try to manipulate
it.
We build piers with dams, reservoirs and canals.
We harvest hydroelectric and tidal power,
build swimming pools and diving playgrounds…
but we're never fully in control.

Water,
the giver of life.
provides fruits from the seas,
takes us to new climes and spreads life on waves.

Water,
the taker of life,
turning from friend to foe in a second.

We can't survive without drinking.
It's the breeding ground for deadly insect disease,
the producer of floods,
trapping us under ice and,
we're only ever one trip from drowning.

H_2O,
the giver and taker of life morphing between
hyperthermia and dehydration,
death and survival.

Always respect water.
Pay homage to Poseidon…
or perhaps you'll have a watery death!

Air

Oxygen from the air in our haemoglobin,
This, the elixir of life that moves our muscles,
keeps us alive.

We have an innate nature to be quizzical about
flight,
to do the impossible as we see feathery friends
glide gracefully,
humans, restricted to the ground kiwi like,
dreaming of soaring like an eagle,
experiencing freedom in three dimensions.

But with gravitational escapism comes danger,
Icarus, carried on the wind,
the sun doing for him.

Wind,
the giver of life,
carrying seeds to new grounds.
Man blown on sails to new lands,
new opportunities,
new beginnings.

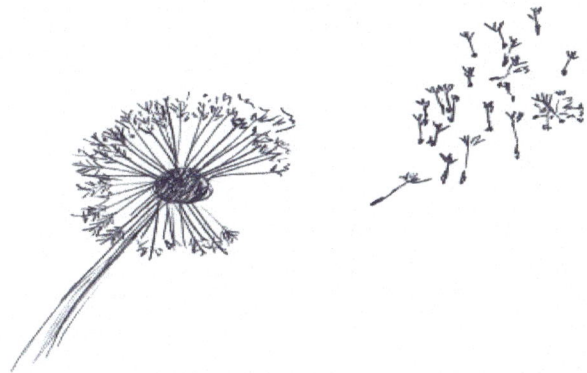

Wind,
the harbinger of death and destruction,
the unimaginable power of tornadoes, typhoons
and hurricanes that pull up trees like twigs,
fling cars like paper cups.

Oxygen,
air and wind,
constructive and destructive forces,
the givers and takers of life,

flight,
rebirth and death.

Give praise,
give thanks;
always respect the elements.

Earth

Soil through my hamds,
life through my limbs,
this is elemental,
where we come from and go to,
earth now decomposing,
subtracting,
not lying,
no one can't escape the truth.

From where we build,
flat or hill,
we are connected to the earth,
life rebirth,
this is understanding.

From whence we come we will go,
back to the earth...
this inevitability,
smoke or buried,
ashes or coffin,
back to the earth whether fast or slow.

Fire, water, air, earth,
the essentials to live,
the building blocks of life,
the harbingers of death.

Human Engineering

Am I a runner or slow jogger?
certainly no athlete!
But that matters little,
running is being human,
it's our nature.

I don't need to be competitive like in other parts
of my life,
but run because I can,
it's my DNA...
PlayStation is not.

I don't need to be the first to cross the line,
I don't even need a line to cross.
The wind in my hair,
the earth moving beneath my feet,
the world passing me by going at my own sweet
pace,
in my own sweet time…
this, my prize!

The joy is running itself,
my body working in unison,
muscles in synergy propelling me across the
ground one stride at a time.

Whether I'm sprinter,
jogger or plodder,
the simple truths are the same:
I run for pleasure of my soul,
to know what my body is capable of,
to test my endurance,
mental as much physical;
I run because running is what my body is engi-
neered to do.

Rugby

Rugger bugger.
Chasing an egg.
A thug's game played by gentlemen.
Banter between supporters and treat officials
with respects.
Gobbledygook to an unbeliever…
colour and passion to the fan.
Rugby,
the greatest sport on earth.

This day marked in my mental calendar,
two hours with friends,
supping a beer or ten;
the camaraderie of bothers-in-arms on the pitch
and in the bar.

Five, four, three, two, one,
the whistle blown,
the ball kicked high.

A ruck, a maul,
jumping in the lineout,
shoving in the scrum,
a try from a pushover,
a field length score.

Half-time,
the match out of control;
get a round of drinks and keep the faith.

The second-half underway,
score from the kick-off.
Smile back on face,
the match can still be won

Ambition

I've put on two stone in two years.
I eat less but still add weight;
a cruel irony in this image obsessed world.

Exercise,
what I enjoy doing,
enjoyed doing has stopped;
my metabolism gone from fast to slow,
muscle replaced with fat,
I'm in a stew.

It's not that I have a wound to my body,
but an injury to my time,
my mind,
my mental health.

I wake at 6,
get the kids ready for school,
drop them and go to work;
back home at 7 for the family evening meal.

Exhausted,
I sit in front of the telly and put feet up;
this all I want,
all I'm capable of doing.

I miss exercising,
doing what I used to enjoy:
flying down a hill on my bike,
hiking up a mountain,
running through the forest.

The only thing I find now…
excuses and bigger clothes!

But today I'm dressed in shorts,
t-shirt and trainers.

I'm excited for new sights,
motivated to know how far I can go,
waiting to be exhilarated,
exhausted,
find out how fast I can run.

I close the door,
keys in pocket,
headphones on and step onto the street.

I look left and right,
take a lungful of oxygen,
place one leg in front of the other,
repeat.

I'm moving quicker than a walk,
slower than the chasing dog.

I turn onto a path,
the park 500 metres away,
my legs feeling good,
breathing easy,
belly wobbling.

I go
and go,
and go,
breathing no longer regular,
wheezing,
legs heavy,
pain on my shin,
stitch in my stomach,
head spinning.

I walk,
ambitions shattered as I stumble,
fumble my way through the park gates.

Walking

Water bottle filled,
walking boots laced,
music jacked,
exercise here I come.

As I walk,
I internal mind talk,
show I have persistence,
perseverance,
and can go through pain barriers,
mind alterations.

Nothing can stop me physically if I'm unstoppa-
ble mentally,
the two,
one and the same,
the similarities,
the differences,
the fortitude needed for both.

This is why I walk,
to know that I can,
to continue when I feel like stopping,
that I am the engine in my life,
can make the alterations needed.

By putting one foot in front of another,
I change the equation,
expectation,
no longer predetermination,
I the exception.

By walking,
I remind myself thus.

Ugly Duckling

Helmet on,
lycra tight,
shoes clanking,
chain greased,
seat adjusted,
lights turned on,
I'm good to go;
once more swan rather than ugly duckling.

I glide on the flat,
fly downhill,
pant on climbs while questioning my sanity;
I'm once more swan rather than ugly duckling.

No swimming or hiking for me,
I need wind on my face,
rain to whip my eyes and sting my skin;
I pedal furiously,
once more swan rather than ugly duckling.

Cycling is my second nature and first love.
I'll leave the house and ride to the pub car park,
the start and end point to my ride,
a comradely pint for this ugly duckling who's
briefly a swan.

15 Miles Per Hour

Bike on I get,
cycle do I go,
move that is the point,
glide I hope… as I watch the world go by 15
miles per hour.

Red light I stop,
park I enter,
trees I pass,
couples I glance… as I watch the world go by 15
miles per hour.

Bend I come to,
lycra I see,
I am flying,
up in the air… as I watch the world go by 15
miles per hour.

Back to earth landing,
face planting,
blood dripping,
bruises hurting,
mouth dirt spitting,
wheel still spinning no longer watching the world
go by 15 miles per hour.

TOURIST OR TRAVELLER, EXPLORING THE WORLD

When you go abroad, whether for work or pleasure, you will go as either tourist or traveller. Whether traveller or tourist, the distinction between the two, subjective. Some proudly proclaim themselves travellers rather than mere tourists. For many, this precious time away, one week from everyday lives, represents a chance for escapism. Whether seeking tranquillity or endless banter, it offers respite from the struggles of minimum wage jobs, zero-hour contracts, austerity and the disenfranchisement of politics.

To explore new lands, whether modern-day Sodom and Gomorrah's or some me time, indulging in a good book, exploring nature through hiking or forging connections with new faces, you will likely need a passport. It's funny to reflect on how the power of a simple document, a few pieces of paper stuck together with glue and tucked within a shiny cover, can be a gateway to new worlds. It's easy to take this privilege for granted, those less fortunate simply not having the chance to fly to the destination of their choice. Similarly, credit cards are a financial lifeline. In any other setting, for instance up a mountain or in a desert, these two relatively innocuous items would be useless, yet, in the context of travel, they become transformative and can shape the trajectory of our lives with new worlds uncovered, horizon broadened, food tasted, sounds listened to and conversations had. Wherever you go, your surroundings will evolve through new landscapes and cultural differences… though the prevalence of the English Premier League is likely to be a constant.

After your trip, a week in the sun or up a mountain, will life go back to the everyday or will there have been a profound life transformation? Will voodoo statues become your new norm? To the possibility of new adventures and the unknown, I say, where is my passport and credit card?

7 Days

Fifty-one weeks.
Three hundred and fifty-eight days.
Eight thousand five hundred and ninety-two
hours until the next escape,
the elixir at the end of the production line,
the office,
stuck at home,
climbing the greasy pole.

One week,
two weeks,
all the piggybank can afford.

Last minute madness or planning all year,
escapism,
escaping the everyday where all things are possible,
fantasies interchangeable,
reality left far behind.

Spend, splurge,
suck, fuck,
dive, dance,
will you enjoyment overload?
before back to banality,
holiday finality,
fifty-one more weeks of mental brutality.

But for those seven days you can be a tourist or
traveller.
To some they are the same,
others, splitting hairs,
a pretentious question.
Yet, to the tourist they are not travellers,
and travellers hate being called tourists.

Who cares about labels when you're seeing the world?
Play on the beach in the morning,
see historical ruins in the afternoon,
go nightclubbing till early hours;
all of the above,
none of the above,
living a different life.

Go on a cruise, a road trip,
a hiking holiday, a biking tour,
coach or horse trekking;
stay in one place or watch the world pass by.

Go to the mountains,
stay in the cities,
swim in rivers, lakes and seas,
chase butterflies in fields as you do what your
heart desires.

Go with friends and family.
Have me time or make new friends;
It's your holiday,
do as you please.

See elephants, sharks, tigers.
Go twitching.
Climb the highest peak.
Run an ultra-marathon.

Enthuse passions and live dreams,
as life is for living,
experiencing,
seeing the world,
imbibing different cultures,
tasting different food,
hearing different music,
speaking different languages and meeting differ-
ent people…
traveller or
tourist?
who cares!

Butterflies

Did I remember my passport, ticket and money?
Is immigration going to be a problem?
Is luggage going to turn up?
Am I going to be lost forever like those on
Malaysian, Lion, Ethiopian Airlines and German
Wings?

Will the next hours, days and weeks,
be the best or worse of my life?
Will I make friends?
What adventures await me?
Will I be on return flight by myself?

No problems checking in,
no aftershave or nail scissors thrown into the
dangerous items bin.
Passports stamped,
time for one last coffee.

Peruse duty free,
rush to boarding gate,
queue slow moving,
watch ticking ever closer to lift-off,
butterflies getting going thinking about door
opening at 37,000 feet.

Bags and jacket overhead locker,
no movies grab my attention.
Pick up newspaper,
start reading,
open novel words not understanding;
need anything for butterfly distracting.

The plane taxis,
runway,
lights ahead glisten,
engines roaring,
calm on my face but chewing gum faster,
butterflies, now gut busting.

I take of,
give silent prayer,
into the unknown I go.
Pinned back in seat,
feel the acceleration,
future out of hands.
close eyes and hope butterflies start sleeping.

Alone

I'm at the airport and leaving love behind.

Travelling can be revitalising,
life affirming,
kick-assing,
but, this time don't know if I'll fly like an eagle or
be a grounded ostrich style,
head in sand?

Soon to enter new city,
start new life,
become a new me,
born again into the world of the living.

New challenges are really opportunities as I ex-
plore the day and night,
form new friendships
hopefully discover heavenly bodies.

I shall live for the now not worry about the mor-
row.
I'll forget the past not be consumed by what I'm
running from.

There will be no shared experiences,
only selfies.
I will have no one who understands me,
who I can adore,
who I can share treasured moments with.

I will be alone in my new reality,
experience the world singularity.
No encumbrances holding me back…
no one gliding with.

I will have no constraints nor companionship.
I will go where I want,
do as I please,
no need to compromise…
but, I won't appreciate my lover's joy.

Soon enough,
I fear,
new will become old,
excitement replaced by repetition.
I will chase the dragon of the always new,
excitement becoming warring,
tiring,
boring,
tear staining.

I will drink to forget my solitude,
my uncertain future,
my loneliness;
while others may assume I'm celebrating I'll really
be drowning my sadness,
mine the tears of a clown.

94 Minutes and 3 Seconds

Take cold beer from the fridge,
pour into icy glass;
I'm dying from humidity.

Take frigid shower,
down tequila shot,
getting ready for tonight.

Shorts and sandals,
aftershave and toothpaste,
I'm good to go.

Right out the flat,
a vodka at the bottlestore;
I'm just getting started.

Catch a tuk-tuk,
weave through traffic,
second destination approaching.

Lie on the table,
have a massage;
benefits included.

Pants on, shorts up,
pay my $20;
another tequila.

Walk on,
destination in mind;
detour via beach bar.

A game of pool,
two beers;
the night starting to fly.

94 minutes and 3 seconds later…
destination reached,
pints start flowing,
girls looking radiant,
the party now starting.

Embassies

We travel to experience new language,
new music,
new food and new people…
but whether north, east, south or west,
home is best.

Being abroad,
tourist or living,
you're a foreigner in a distant land,
a fish out of water…
an embassy,
a little piece of home,
of the familiar.

To return to all you once knew,
took for granted,
is not easy emotionally, physically or legally –
consular services are needy.

Embassy officials,
civil servants with a civil servant mind-set who
wear holiday clothes.

They are admin pushing,
paperwork loving,
law abiding,
defending the rules types.
They dot the I's and cross the t's,
do this don't do that, their hymn.

Endless instructions given,
processes incomprehensible.
Don't do this can't do that,
you're told from the other side of a glass divide as
frustrations boil over.

Embassies,
the familiar,
where you're not a foreigner in a foreign land,
but, a little piece of home,
there to help in times of distress;
when you're in need,
embassies are an awkward though necessary
friend indeed.

New Adventure

2,000 kilometres from home,
life,
this a voyage of self-discovery,
soul-recovery.

Will this be a journey of loneliness or new
friendships,
new lovers,
new meaning to the life I left behind?

I'll be exploring surroundings,
reaching the deepest recesses of my being,
ruminating,
defining what made me,
what makes me,
what will define me going forwarding.

I have no answer,
no personal solution,
no plan or preconceptions,
but will go with the flow,
play it by ear and be led by serendipity.

Will these weeks transform or inform,
bore or I'll live life galore?
Will I repent,
forgive myself and others as I mind explore.

After this experience,
experiment,
what will life look like?
Will I be changed by one more entry on my life
reality?

Berlin

I came to Berlin last weekend,
blown away by the vibe
the freedoms,
people being who they are,
no false personas,
pretension,
discrimination,
police intimidation.

It's a city that's alive,
crackling with adventure,
creativity,
uniqueness,
superlatively.

A month ago,
I flew into Tegal,
life,
now one of more and less.

More festivals,
more drinks,
more temporary friends,
one night stands,
more spliffs… less work,
less mornings without a hangover,
less savings…
more impossibly cool bars,

first time experiences,
but with less of a girlfriend,
less of a property I call my own,
less mental stability.

Three months and the German capital is my
home for today,
tomorrow,
hopefully forever.

The gloss is fading,
but I still love the spirit,
the, anything is possible on a night out…
but making a new life is tiring,
soul searching,
Euro consuming.

Finding new friends,
starting a new job,
moving from rented accommodation to
house-sharing,
always hoping for love finding,
I moving party to party while becoming ever
more lonely;
it's not so great to relocate!

I've been here a year…
the scooters and bikes littering the streets annoy me,
those I thought friends,
deserted me.

I'm living,
but on the breadline,
no more headline,
no more edgy adventures.
I dance the fandango till dawn as I have no one
to share a bed with.
Berlin,
nights all ending in foggy-eyed loneliness;
you promised much but have taken more.

I will never leave Berlin my home for fifteen years.
This is where I found true friends in my first 15 days,

where I can be who I want,
but, what I want is normality,
a family to call my own,
children not just mates.

Berlin, I still love you.
I admire all you stand for,
but, I'm more cynical.
Interesting characters make unreliable friends.
A sharing economy only enriches entrepreneurs.
Too much partying leads to financial instability,
mental fallibility,
happiness temporarily. .

Berlin,
you're a cold bitch!
I respect you and love your self-preservation,
your promises to the wild-eyed and free of heart
are immense…
the way you consume and spit out fresh meat,
hope…
now I know this is your secret to continue the
cycle of creativity,
of living,
breathing,
surviving
thriving…
of being Berlin.

East Side Gallery

Twelve to the day,
a birthday surprise like no other,
an erection of utmost dejection,
rejection,
understanding and empathy.

The 13th August, 1961,
a Sunday with families on holidays,
Berlin,
quiet apart from church bells and army trucks.

Barbed wire unveiled.
fences erected and bridges sealed.
Hearts and families ripped apart,
destruction of hope start,
the city of souls and new destinies designed and
forged now patrolled by machine-gun.

Tunnels soon dug,
canals swam,
guards dodged,
power lines tightropes,
freedom taken and lives lost.

This construction of obstruction,
intrusion,
confusion,
site of execution…

is now reflection,
humanity and expectation.

30 years after the wall was built,
now torn down.
The site of destruction,
now contemplation,
where life's reviewed,
friendships renewed.

This East Side Gallery,
a place for celebration,
symbol of reunification,
artistic expression,
the country reborn,
smiles not scorn,
hope no longer forlorn.

City of Contrasts

Berlin,
a city of contrasts,
freedom and rules,
norms and the unnatural,
the socially acceptable,
where anything goes as long as it's within the
lines Mr Squiggle drew so random are they to the
uninitiated.

Booze flows from every grocery store,
consume where you want,
so much revelry…
but little drunkenness,
no police,
joy to impinge;
they, not needed,
there's no lawlessness.

Drugs sold on corners,
in many nightclubs,
openly,
freely,
everyone getting smoked
coked,
enjoying on the street.

Fuck who you want,
where and when you want-
in swingers club
dogging,
the kino;
prostitution is legal,
DildoKing the prince,
monarch of the billboards…

But don't whisper outside a bar if there's live
music;
you'll get told off.

Don't step into a cycle lane or cross the road
when red Jesus is showing.

Wearing a rucksack on a tram,
great potential for tutting and scorn.

Don't download torrents or you'll be fined.

There are rules unknown:
bouncers,
the gatekeepers to hedonism,
their whim,
prerogative,
deciding who's entering.

Berlin,
a city of contrasts;
rules of law and culture,
those enforced not what you expect.

Herman the German

German talking,
sauerkraut eating,
beer chugging,
fräulein tits sucking;
Herman's my man and enjoying life.

Engineer measuring,
orphanage opening,
big dick walking,
he's living with a purpose;
Herman's my man and enjoying life.

Always believing,
BMW driving,
Mercedes scorning,
Munich to the bone;
Herman's my man and enjoying life.

Bayern watching,
Oom-pah blowing,
Oktoberfest puking,
always up for the craic;
Herman's my man and enjoying life.

Red Jesus

I'm walking from here to there,
A to B via C,
no destination in mind
no date with destiny or somewhere to find,
just wandering,
my immediate future,
only fate knows what's in store.

I pick up my pace,
the minute hand circling,
the blue dot,
me,
moving.

Look left,
look right,
don't get flattened,
receive angry staring

back of the head slapping,
words of incomprehension for my stupidity,
incomprehending.

I'm not talking road crossing...
It would be expected drivers venting,
red mist showing.

This is not at a sport stadium,
frustrated fans jostling to the front of the que,
the best seat.

This is not in a pub or club,
joviality,
where camaraderie reigns
but punch-ups begin.

No,
this is the mean streets of Berlin,
the pavements of palaver.

The two-wheeler menace,
the bike,
bicycle,
occasional tricycle is king of designated lanes.

Anyone crossing their line,
onto hallowed turf,
better be travelling at speed...
or looking left then right.

Bicycles whiz past,
the yellow tram I could have taken stopping
ahead,
too far before it pulls out.
I could jog but don't want sweaty mess.

Come to traffic lights,
the red man,
Jesus who must be obeyed showing,
glowing.

It's impossible,
man on foot,
bike or car to disobey him;
that would be inexcusable,
blasphemous...
but today I will not be stopped,
delayed,
not even by the little red man,
even if I get verbally crucified.

A pagan foreigner,
I take the plunge,
the green man with erect phallus not yet showing.

With life in hands...
I walk the empty street,
no car or tram in sight as I road crossing,

Germans look at me with unveiled disgust,
I rule breaking,
their eyes questioning.

The Polizei,
blue and silver car in front pulling,
lights flashing,
they chasing major criminal I thinking...
before receiving a surprising fining.

Ich bin ein Berliner

I'm a punk,
a Berliner and this is my home.
I wear my hair in mohawk,
chains, army boots and denim my ensemble.

I'm Vietnamese,
a Berliner and this is my home.
I work in restaurant with my family,
see business opportunities and a better life for
my children.

I'm a drag queen,
a Berliner and this is my home.
I wear what I want,
accepted for who I am,
strangers as unconcerned by my choices as
friends.

I'm a university student,
a Berliner and this is my home.
I'm starting the life experience,

the future unknown;
I will make life what I dare.

I'm a business owner
a Berliner and this is my home.
I own a million Euro flat and drink on the street.
I drive my Porsche, ride my electric bike and par-
ty at Bergheim when it pleases.

I'm a bouncer,
a Berliner and this is my home.
I allow others to have fun,
but I control this city of few rules;
my nightclub, my house, my whim.

I'm a family man
a recent arrival to Berlin,
this my new home.
I work in an office,
The children adjusting to a new culture,
language and school system,
these all new norms to living in Berlin.

I'm part of the LGBTQ+ community,
a Berliner and this is my home.
I love who my heart desires and can walk hand-
in-hand with my partner, best friend or spouse in
confidence.

I'm Polizei,
a Berliner and this is my home.
I'm a friend when in need…
but let people lead their lives,
my city ruling itself through respect.

I'm a refugee,
a recent Berliner,
here, my new home.
My skin and voice similar to many I pass in im-
migrant communities,
these my new neighbours.

I'm a tattooist,
a Berliner and this is my home.
Ink is my life,
Berliner's bodies my canvas.

I'm here on holidays,
to see the sights,

imbibe the culture and dance the nights away.
Where I live I'm not accepted for who I am or
my life choices.
I'm not free or able to live in peace.
I'm not a Berliner but wish I lived here.

Languages

Lived a dozen countries,
travelled a million more.
Can't speak a word of Finnish,
Spanish or Timbuktuish...

Not speaking the local lingo,
remiss,
but not vital to earn my bread,
pay my rent, live.

I put mental energy where I need to focus,
English my mother tongue,
the people I talk to,
professionals I work with,
whether Pacific, Africa or the Stans,
all know it.

It would be better,
an advantage to know some words
but I have to decide and make compromises,
I'm ok with that.

Road Trip

Wake at 7,
not slept a wink,
too much on my mind.

Contemplate a wank,
don't have the energy,
not even inclination.

Watch a film,
finish last night's pizza;
long day ahead.

To the matatu,
print my visa;
soon on my way.

Morning sun burns,
border by lunchtime;
apparently, I overstayed.

Find a ride,
unsuccessful haggle,
beady eyes on suitcase.

The hours drag,
towns are passed,
traffic becomes claustrophobic.

It's dark now,
no idea where I am;
fate in the hand of the gods.

Pillion with jumbo suitcase,
rough roads and crazy drivers,
hand on heart.

Follow a fellow passenger,
destination found,
sleep above a nightclub.

Need one or two,
more like three or four,
just another day in the life of…

Hear familiar crack,
spy pool cues;
this, the start of new adventures.

The Combustion Engine

I get keys to my future,
to independence,
to life…
to my Suzuki Vitara.

14 years and two versions old,
I'm ecstatic about the endless possibilities.

No more trains, buses
or borrowing the car from mum;
this is my chick magnet,
my shaggin' wagon.

Never mind 0-60,
the Green Lantern is a teleporting machine…
transporting me from mundane existence to new
lives,
to freedom,
to life.

TOURIST OR TRAVELLER, EXPLORING THE WORLD

Mind the Gap

London,
the world's mixing pot of colours, creeds and
religions,
a city of unending possibilities,
people being what they want,
living life as they see fit.

The crowded Underground,
the rainbow lines connections of my life that fuse
my past to present,
a gateway to my future.

At Hammersmith I go to discuss partnership to a
posse of potential partners.
Alighting near the Lyric Theatre,
granola for breakfast at a small café before
talking business,
agreeing partnership frameworks and next steps.

Shepherds Bush welcomes me with colour, smells
and the noise of the market,
a rich array of stimuli flooding my senses.
As I walk along Uxbridge Road I turn to the left,
walk five minutes to my destination,
my dying Auntie's house.

I walk to White City and get on the Central Line.
I cross the capital to the Square Mile,
change onto Docklands Light Railway and alight
at Canary Wharf to see an old school friend,
a successful banker.

It's early evening,
commuters going home complaining about ex-

pensive house prices and ticket prices,
Groups of friends go into the West End;
now I'm on the Piccadilly Line to Heathrow.

The stations and tubes are overcrowded,
this is true,
not the grandiose Moscow or artistic metro in
Helsinki…
but the London Underground represents family
and friends,
loves and lovers,
work and business opportunities,
high success and dismal failure.

As the tube did for my yesteryear it has done for
my today.
I'm grateful to the hymn,
"Mind the Gap";
it has engaged me with my past,
it's the starting gun to my future.

AFRICA

Africa's post-independence trajectory has witnessed shifts from Soviet socialist ideals to the embrace of corrupt capitalism, this leaving many citizens to bear the brunt of their leaders' self-enrichment. I'm all for self-rule but at what cost when many citizens are hood-winked into poverty in the shadow of the lavish lives of politicians and elite? That citizens want change, peaceful or otherwise, at home or via immigration, is not a surprise!

You may recognise the above, but what do you really know of Africa? It's a continent of 54 countries, 2 billion+ people and my home for 17 years? It's crucial to go beyond the stereotypes and assumptions, though I expect words that comes to your mind, include famine, Bono, refugees, Geldof, Archbishop Desmond Tutu, Didier Drogba, Mo Salah (Egypt is in Africa), mystery, ebony babes, Arab Spring, Table Top Mountain, safari, hakuna matata (the Lion King) Suez Canal, blood diamonds, youth, floods and draughts, civil war and coup to mention but a few. But what do you really know of the continent other than what you've been told? Are your pre-conceptions, formed over a lifetime, about seeing half-naked men carrying spears and wearing the carcasses of their kills? What about women with clay pots perched on their heads and breasts swinging in the sea-breeze as they go from mud-hut to tin-shack while fly-infested children with bug-like eyes (from dysentery and malnutrition) listlessly look on? This is a very limited perspective. It's important to challenge preconceived notions and explore the truth of the continent, as the reality, Africa is a place of immense richness and complexity. It's true that in rural areas and urban slums there's extreme poverty, but, many cities are fast growing metropolises with construction cranes dotting the skyline. People wear pretty much the same as me. In all honesty, if anything, at times I'm a little disappointed at the mundane life that seems not so very different from the UK or other parts of the developed world, albeit with different challenges, more heat and less money. To truly understand Africa, one must engage with its history, cultures, people, and contemporary realities. It's a continent that defies simplistic narratives but rather offers a wealth of stories and experiences waiting to be explored beyond surface-level misconceptions.

Mistress Africa

Africa,
Africans,
the dark continent full of dark bodies,
a wasteland,
a stain on the human conscience,
wars and genocide,
nepotism and corruption,
kleptomaniac leaders,
a blight on humanity…

Ever a good news story from those cursed lands?
Any sliver of hope among the destitution?
What words would you describe where my heart
is,
the birth place of my children,
the land of my reawakening?

Youth and entrepreneurism?
Freedom?
Living a life less connected?

Africa is my mistress and she calls me back to her
bosom.
It's a question of when not if I chase my dream,
follow my destiny and rekindle my love with her.

Africa,
where contradictions are everyday:
beautiful women with bad wigs,
phones cordless,
leaders clueless,
youth jobless,
children motherless,
banks cashless,
and the list goes on…

this everything I love,
everything I miss.

My heart is not at peace in the UK,
the land I once called home,
where repetition and order rule,
where there is no annoyance at the unpredictable,
no life elixir.

I don't always know what I'm looking for…
but feeling encased here;
being claustrophobic is not living,
I miss feeling alive!

My true love,
my mistress Mother Africa is calling me back.

Two Faces

The City Face

An ocean city
paradise,
a sea breeze that
refreshes when
having a sun-downer,
it's so easy to unwind
over chat and drink
anytime of the week.

As I look across
perfect sandy beaches
and watch the surf break,
I watch sea eagles glide on air currents and dolphins playing in the distance,
the humidity and traffic is forgotten,
the weight of the world lifted from shoulders.

It's a truly magical experience,
but life's not a utopia.
You get screwed for this or that,
are forced to pay ignorance tax when you don't
know the right palms to grease.
It's a fast life with fast people –
opportunists always looking for a quick buck.

The Rural Face

My child's sick,
what do I do?
Travel to the clinic,
but what if there's no doctor?

It's thirty kilometres,
a three-hour minibus ride which I can't afford as
the crop this year failed,
an eight-hour walk in the blistering sun…
my child will never manage.

And even if I get there I can't buy the medicine!
I can go without food but my other children
can't;
one meal a day can't be cut to zero,
they will starve.

My baby is getting weaker,
fever ravishing her innocent body.
Cheeks are gaunt,
skin clammy,
eyes discoloured,
slipping from this world,
peace for her fragile life only hours away.

I have to try,
I can't sit by and do nothing.

I gather what little money I have,
the father,
my husband,
drunk,
spending our few pennies whoring.

I explain to her siblings,
"Tonight, no food."
They know their sister is dying,
they happily go without,
their tummies rumbling,
bellies protruding,
malnourished,
they born into poverty.

Bus conductor paid,
I pray to God wishing the wheels turn quicker,
the city coming into view as my daughter slips
into the next life.

A Fridge Rich in Commercial Aid (AFRICA)

Beauty all around,
the lands of sugar and honey,
unblemished,
not touched since the beginning of time.

Many are jealous of what they don't have:
cameras and cars,
mansions and skyscrapers,
money…
but,
should they want the consequences?
Murder and rape,
theft and offence,
hassles and danger,
stress over money troubles.

Questions rightfully asked,
include,
is the west under-developing Africa?
Is there hypocrisy in western democracy?
Is aid a mask for economic colonisation?

Development money is a pittance compared to
interest on national debt,
to family remittances,
to western tariff barriers;
aid,
a pretty marketing face with a rotten economic
soul.

Africa is a fridge full of natural resources…
but there are corrupt hands,
greedy,
selfish people who take the nation's wealth,
who take from those with little.

And yet the people have not been corrupted.
Family values and respect for elders is present,
children are seen and heard,
there is welcoming of strangers and community
spirit,
laughter and hope ring out throughout the community.

Mother Africa holds my soul.

Africa

The continent
largely peaceful but with rumblings of discontent.
Africa,
a new Wild West where I feel alive,
why I'm here,
as I want to dare,
to be challenged,
to know what's possible and what I'm capable of.

I want to uncover,
understand my motivations for being here,
from running from what I know.

I want to search for success and no longer fear failure;
Mother Africa gives me this present.

I don't want to leave,
but…
should I stick or twist in this land of opportunity and uncertainty?
Will I get screwed or make a million?
What does fate have in-store?

The Market

Fifty metres past the church,
left down muddy track,
charcoal and DVD vendors on my flanks,
the stench of rain and open drains in my nostrils.

Space opens up,
the market,
a kaleidoscope of colours,
noises and smells;
it's a sensory overload.

A cavalcade of bars down one side where music blasts through broken speakers,
salons and barber shops down the other;
the hubbub all encompassing.
I enter like Daniel into the den-
watermelon, mango, lettuce, garlic, tomato, potato –
each with their perfume,
each their negotiation.

An extra kilo of that,
two less of these.

Keep to my budget,
haggling culture part of the fun going to the market.

We leave,
shoulders straining,
content in the knowledge I'll be feasting on freshness till next week's visit to the market.

A Slice of Peace

I leave my $7.50 a night pension,
walk cobbles streets,
past belching taxis,
young and old beggars,
open sewers,
prostitutes standing on the corner,
all the while thinking of the night ahead.

It's a Wednesday evening,
sunny but chilly,
jumper in the rucksack,
bottle soon to lips,

As I wander I ponder,
remember where I've come from and going to,
figuratively and literally,

Pass the long que waiting for the cramped mini-
bus,
hardware shops, their wares on the roadside,
coffee huts six at a time.

I continue,
destination in mind,
pollution,
noise and bustle my companions.

Rushed and sweaty,
I reach the 5-star hotel,
world renowned luxury.

Inside, a cornucopia of skin colours and languag-
es,
business moguls,
princes and high-class hookers all relaxing in
splendid comfort;
this entitlement,
part of my reality but not totality.

I see lonely souls in this quiet corner of paradise
where everybody has everything,
where wins are taken for granted.

I've stayed such places many times.
It's very comfortable,
relaxing.
I'm treated well...
but a beer, double my tonight bed fee,
though money is not the issue for current accom-
modation choices.

I talk to a Canadian, Russian and Syrian,
we all foreigners in a foreign country,
not knowing the here or respective homes where
loved ones remain,
where friends laugh without you,
where life ticks from this hour to the next,
the seasons passing.

Tonight feels a time-warp of hope and failure,
challenge and success.
I'm making it through the day,
doing what I need,
with who I need,
to survive,
thrive,
not knowing if I made the right decision to leave,
to take a chance on life,
of throwing my hat in the ring of the unknown,
of living in this African metropolis.

The Black Rose of Africa

Tanzania,
the melting pot of Africa.
Arab and African in harmony,
Christians and Muslims in peace.
Language, looks, food, music;
a combination of influences over centuries.

Old Tanzania,
a one-party state,
Nyerere,
like many a strong man of Africa,
tyranny dressed up as benevolence.

Modern Tanzania,
a cosmopolitan capital with nightclubs and
lounges,
beggars and bureaucrats,
diplomats and market traders,
farmers and businessmen all mingling,
living side-by-side,
some in the fast lane…
many left behind.

There are highways,
shiny busways,
wanting to be the pride of the airways,
but still mainly dusty country byways,
people urinating down alleyways.
Strict immigration and ever-present police.
Fake pastors and mosques by the dozen.

Girls on street corners and massage parlours
galore.

This is a rejuvenated economy of disputed dem-
ocratic leadership -
there are growth and transformation plans,
this leading to socio-economic gap widening.

Tanzania,
a land of contradictions,
the black rose of Africa.

Malawi

Malawi,
the Warm Heart of Africa,
the confusion of my future.

A land of opportunity and uncertainty;
get screwed or make a million?

Corruption and Cashgate,
the country for sale.

Peaceful, but with limited economy;
moving forward at a lackadaisical pace.

The few rich getting richer,
the masses left behind.

Malawi,
the Warm Heart of Africa,
a land of contrasts.

Ethiopia

On the lake,
small plane arrive,
finish work,
want to party.

Drink beer,
play pool.
Given a fish,
help a small boy.
Find a friend,
shit with no loo roll.

Island monasteries and cheap hookers;
traditional nightclubs with fuck rooms in the
back.

Feel lonely so keep busy,
walk and edit,
search my soul and come to conclusions:
I miss my wife,
my kids.

See good looking girls,
bitches,
they want money only,
no idea who I am,

what I'm up to,
make up with no substance,
guaranteed turbulence,
no common sense...

Do what I do,
not feel compelled,
drink for courage,
to forget,
to have hope of finding a same heart,
to brush past desperation,
depression.

I will continue on,
move forward
keep my shit together one day at a time
some days easier than others.

My time here is finished.
I've learnt more about who I am and what I
want,
what I have and what I don't.
The next city,
country,
another mental challenge,
experience on my reality

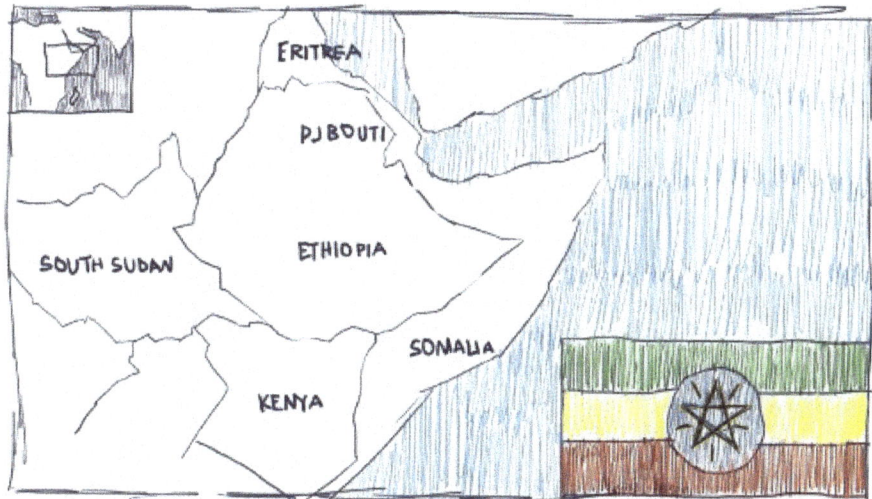

61

We are Habesha

Born in the same continent but not of the same
soul.
We are the chosen people;
we are habesha.

We have a strong history,
a proud culture.
We are not African, but Ethiopian.
Fuck you Roman calendar, food and language-
we are God's people,
African Israelites;
Ethiopia,
the promised land where the tabernacle settles.

We are a mix of African and Arab,
of history and modernity.
Never colonized,
bastardised,
but Ethiopian,
11 regions together,
Federal, but culturally unique.

We are religion and being free,
Christians and Muslims side-by-side.
We make our own rules,
dance, sing and rejoice unique.
We take the best of all,
we create cultural beauty;
we are Habesha.

COVID-19

I'm a tour guide,
handsome and smart,
friendly,
good at English,
husband and father.

I've tried my best,
followed the rules,
made my independent way in life.

COVID-19 fucked me!

I'm not sick,
my family all well but income dried up.
No tourists means no food for my baby,
my pregnant wife going hungry,
nothing to send to my parents.

I,
who got the furthest with education,
the good job and lush house,
have the greatest responsibility,
accountability,
I, the one who everyone depends on,
looks up to.

I have to provide,
this is what I know,
what is expected of me.

I do what I can but have no furlough,
no unemployment benefits...
like my foreigner clients.
My options...
bus driver if I'm lucky,
army if desperate.

I cry out of shame,
the desperation of my livelihood,
my family's hope being taken away.

Living is out of my control while a new life of
my seed is born.

Zanzibar

Zanzibar,
an ocean paradise of political tension,
frustration,
citizens wanting vindication.

I walk the alleyways and stop at random cafes.
I'm lost,
knowing not nor caring where I go,
where I will end up.

I detour to the beach,
watch the surf break,
feel the sea breeze refresh me from this week as a
sundowner eases me into the night.

It's a magical experience,
the weight of the world lifting from my shoul-
ders.

Now I want a few,
poems a lot as I walk the unknown seafront,
thinking of the night,
not sure what to come,
no expectations or limitations,
but hope.

See flashing lights,
hear karaoke,
joy and festivity,
my loneliness fine with this,
not jealous,
but wishing a chat,
a chuckle,
maybe a twist and turn.

Enter,
order a pint,
the vibe not happening for me nor my loneliness.

This is a story I know well,
often travel on own.

It's a game of win some lose some,
don't care about some,
make it more some,
into the night some,
see what will happen some,
this why explore-
who dares wins!

Enter a bar with blue lights,
random choice but music blasting,
girls kissing,
I feeling old,
time passing me by,
temples a greying,
I will not be withering but fight the dying of the
light.

Seven beers in,
one good chat,
two girls talked to.

Back to the road,
into the night unknown.
Twenty metres on from the house of disrepute,
green lights catch my attention,
a curvaceous ass in the doorway the deal maker,
cock agitator.

Enter the bar,
small,
three girls and barman.
Feel at home,
the music rocking,
lyrics foreign,
feels like I'm living.

By a round,
two.
I'm tasting life,
laughing and booty grabbing,

shots pounding,
arms twirling,
top downing,
nipples sucking,
pussy rubbing,

hand grabbing,
shisha smoking,
more beer drinking,
soon panty dropping,
pussy entering;
this, green light celebrating.

Together as One

We are the children of Africa,
born of the same mother,
rise and fall together,
personally and as nations,
leading and being led;
we are children of Africa,
born of the same mother.

We know of each other,
undying,
the underlining truths of our continent,
colonial pasts,
economic colonisation presents.
We are children of Africa,
born of the same mother.

Our story is one of hope,
youth,
entrepreneurship,
trying,
being denied and trying again,
of familial crabs pulling us back down into the bucket,
only a determined few escaping claws.
We are children of Africa,
born of the same mother.

We strive,
plan to thrive,

make it through each day,
power cuts and corruption our reality,
development opportunities not for all.
We are children of Africa,
born of the same mother.

The past of ancestors hangs sway,
the present no one can say,
but the future,
we'll make it our way.
We are all children of Africa,
born of the same mother.

A FINAL THOUGHT

A creative life, whether actor, musician or in my case writer and poet, isn't for everyone. It requires a special kind of dedication and passion. One word that encapsulates this spirit, one of my power words is meraki, a Greek word meaning, to do something creative or artistic with passion. It can be as simple as making a cup of wonderful tea or as complex as crafting a masterpiece. Whatever it is, doing it with absolute love, pleasure and devotion is key. It means putting all your soul into it and doing it with utmost effort, enthusiasm and eagerness, with all your heart. For example, if dancing, move with every fibre of your body, with expression and grace. If cooking, infuse every ingredient with your love; prepare that pasta bolognaise or salad with meraki. If an artist, why not create a whimsical piece like a global map in the shape of a chicken… just for fun. When playing sport, stretch every sinew and push your physical boundaries. If traveling, experience every taste, smell, and sound; explore the unknown with all your senses.

I write novels and poetry with meraki. If you also want to create with the pen or keyboard here are some tips.

1. Write because you can. Understand your motivation. Is it to get the shit out of your head, a minor side income, your love of the written word or, because you want to become a digital nomad? All the above?
2. Break down the insurmountable of your project into the achievable.
3. Give it a twist so it stands out from the crowd.
4. Be authentic otherwise don't bother. Readers can hear and see the writer in their mind's eye; don't bullshit your audience.
5. Read lots and lots and lots, whether blogs, newspapers or novels. Reading is learning and can be a constant source of inspiration.
6. If you are in this for the money, work out a strategy to build followers; you need to hit a tipping-point for financial viability.
7. Keep pounding out regular content. Some say, it should consistently be about the same topics, others advise variety.
8. Leave comments on others' posts and reply to all opinions on yours.
9. Catchy headlines are critical. And if you use photos, always credit the source.
10. Find your meraki, your own voice. This crosses over many of the above points.

I find one of the best ways to find inspiration and creativity is through travelling. Tanzanians, Jordanians and Malawians are quite different in almost every aspect to my previous existence. However, I have come to see and understand people from diverse backgrounds opens my eyes to the common threads of humanity. No matter the country someone comes from, god they worship, gender people lie next to, language that is spoken nor, the colour of someone's skin, there are universal truths that connect us all such as love, communication, empathy, basic freedoms, human rights, friendship, loneliness, uncertainty, judgement, missing friends, being in the minority, open-mindedness, power cuts, cockroaches and mosquitoes. These shared experiences remind me of our collective humanity and provide endless inspiration for creative endeavours.

Thank you, dear reader, my friend for being on this poetic journey. I hope through my experiences I have given you a new perspective on life. So, I say, never blame your circumstances. A positive mind-set will always lead to a more fortuitous outcome than a negative approach. One should not fear failure; it happens- get up and give it another lash. Don't be ashamed of your mistakes; learn from them. We all screw-up, accept this is part of life. Embrace experience, good or bad; there is always something to be learned. If you don't go after what you want, you will never have it. If you don't ask, the answer is always no. If you don't step forward, you will remain in the same place. Be curious and have a willingness to engage with the unknown. Questioning does not show weakness but is rather a sign of strength, a true measure of intelligence. Open yourself to the world and express that you aren't afraid to exhibit your ignorance but want to learn, search for knowledge and truth from those who can educate and guide. "By doubting we are led to question, by questioning we arrive at the truth." Peter Abelard, 1079- 1142

Dancing in the Rain

I'm risking it all as I chase my dream,
my destiny.
With balls in hand,
I dare the consequences.

I'm a gambler,
at stake,
the rest of my life;
if I put my soul into what I believe,
life will sort itself out,
will turn out all right.

12 months,
my first flirtation with Africa and I'm in love;
the smells, colours and people,
a frankness of reality.

Africa is…
living on the edge.
There's poverty,
but with hopeful and happy faces.
It's a humbling contrast to my fortunate upbring-
ing,
here, someone with little can have much more
than another with plenty!

I have seen much and experienced more.
I have lived close to the emotional and financial
edge,
But with strength,
conviction and Africa in my heart,

I will keep chasing my dream,
keep trying to fulfil my potential through feeling
the vivaciousness of life.

Mother Africa,
my love,
my lover,
my siren who calls me.
Africa, you have made me whole,
you have taught me how to dance in the rain.

ABOUT THE AUTHOR

I'm an entrepreneur & business consultant by day, novelist & poet by night. The son of a British Army officer, I volunteered in rural Tanzania in 1997 before going to university to study marketing. I have lived and worked in Ethiopia, Germany, Kenya, Jordan, Ireland, Malawi, Saudi Arabia, Tanzania and the UK over the last 25 years, my varied experiences of culture, relationships, food, music and everything else that makes the world go round, the source of my inspiration.